Lessons in Waiting

A mother's story of hope

ADRIENE DICKERSON

Lessons in Waiting by Adriene Dickerson

© 2017 Adriene Dickerson, LLC

Cover by Erick Pfleiderer. www.pfly.com

ISBN: 1979815852

CreateSpace Independent Publishing Platform

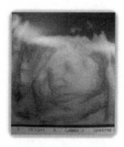

For Adalynn

For you created my inmost being;

you knit me together in my mother's womb.

I praise you because I am fearfully and wonderfully made;

your works are wonderful,

I know that full well.

My frame was not hidden from you

when I was made in the secret place,

when I was woven together in the depths of the earth.

Your eyes saw my unformed body;

all the days ordained for me were written in your book

before one of them came to be.

Psalm 139:13-16

January 13

"Termination is an option," the doctor said softly, "if that is something you would consider."

I shook my head in confusion.

"Of course there are other options as well," he continued quickly, "that they'll go over with you at Children's."

He handed me the phone.

"There is a series of open-heart surgeries they may be able to do, or there is comfort care as another alternative."

I brought the receiver to my ear and heard myself providing my name, address and insurance information to make an appointment for a fetal echocardiogram at Children's National Medical Center in two weeks.

My husband, Adam, was on his cell phone arranging for someone to pick up our daughter at school. Our appointment wasn't supposed to take so long. It was supposed to be a routine sonogram—the day we'd been looking forward to for weeks to find out whether we were having a boy or a girl.

I shook my head again, trying to make everything the doctor had just said somehow go away.

Only an hour before, we had been happily waiting for the exam to begin. I was 18 weeks pregnant with our third child. We were both not so secretly hoping for a boy, but of course gave everyone the standard "as long as it's healthy, either would be perfect" response when questioned on our preference. The scan began as any other. We felt like old pros, having had several ultrasounds when I was pregnant with our two daughters, now ages 7 and 3.

"It's a girl," the sonographer informed us.

A moment of disappointment quickly turned to happiness and excitement. Of course it was a girl. She would be perfect. No matter how we'd tried to convince our daughters just how much fun a little brother would be, they'd insisted they wanted a baby sister. They would be overjoyed.

But the test went on and on.

Our eyes met nervously.

The tech's passive expression gave away nothing as she returned again and again to the baby's heart. She calmly put down the ultrasound wand and asked us to hang tight. The doctor may want to take just a couple more scans, she said, closing the door behind her.

We waited for the doctor, afraid of what we were about to be told. Clearly something was wrong. The doctor said little as he studied the baby's heart and lungs. After a few minutes, he quietly told me I could get dressed; he would wait for us outside.

As I wiped the ultrasound gel off my abdomen, Adam and I looked at each other in bewilderment.

Was there something wrong with her heart?

In his office, the doctor explained that our baby girl had hypoplastic left heart syndrome, HLHS. At the time, this meant nothing to us. It seemed that, for whatever reason, her heart had developed with little or no left ventricle. The baby would be able to grow quite well in utero, he told us, but once she was born, she would not be able to pump blood to her body. Was there any history of congenital heart defects in our families? No? It can occur randomly as well. Sometimes there is no known cause. We would need to go to Children's for further testing to get a more detailed picture of the baby's heart. He assured me she was not in any pain. Fetuses, he said, do not need a left ventricle while they are developing. It

5

is only when the baby is born that this becomes a very serious problem. He was so sorry. Could he get me a glass of water?

Adam and I drove home and held each other in our kitchen for a long time. What would we tell the girls? We called our mothers—each so strong in her faith and confident that God was in control, as always.

We thanked God for our precious baby girl and placed her in His hands. We prayed for a misdiagnosis, a mistake, a miracle.

But the echocardiogram two weeks later confirmed the initial diagnosis. And, as the fetal cardiologist at Children's methodically explained the parts of a normal heart, the parts of a hypoplastic heart, and continued to list other defects—aortic arch hypoplasia, highly restrictive atrial septum—the true severity of what our daughter was facing sunk in. This was not the typical HLHS I had read about as I poured over every related web site, article and blog I could find in the two weeks between my appointments. I had read enough to know that HLHS was very serious, one of the most complex and hardest to manage of all congenital heart defects. But there had been so many amazing advances in the way this disease was treated. Survival rates for babies with HLHS had climbed over the past thirty years from zero to nearly 80%. I had been so hopeful. We'd just go through each of the surgeries: the first at 5-7 days old, the next at six months, the last at eighteen months. Everything would be fine.

Apparently this was not so simple.

The fetal cardiologist described the series of surgeries that would be needed in more detail, pausing as she gave the survival rate statistics for each procedure, to say: "As long as her lungs have not been damaged."

When she finished, I asked her what the survival rate would be if there *were* lung damage.

She looked at me with a mixture of kindness and pity.

"Not so good," she said.

There were just too many factors to know for sure what the outcome would be, she explained, but babies with a restrictive or intact atrial septum are generally very sick when they are born and do not typically do as well as HLHS babies without this additional defect. A C-section at Children's would likely be our best option, so a team of people could be standing by to take the baby to the Cath Lab to try to open up her atrial septum—the wall between the two upper chambers of her heart—immediately after birth.

More tests were needed: follow-up echo-cardiograms, an MRI to see if there were already signs of lung damage. She would consult with a group of specialists at Boston Children's Hospital who had developed techniques for attempting to create an opening in the atrial septum in utero—a fetal cardiac intervention—to see if our daughter was a good candidate for this procedure.

"You're very brave," she told us.

I certainly didn't feel brave.

As we sat in the small conference room that was to become so familiar in the months to come, I didn't cry only because it didn't seem like it would help anything to be hysterical. Crying would change nothing.

Framed newspaper articles adorned the walls, stories of miracle babies that had made it, of parents who had never given up hope. I read the article about a little boy with HLHS and a severely restrictive atrial septum every time I sat there, waiting for the doctor to come in and review the latest tests with us. He was 11 now and liked to play the guitar.

As we drove home from that long afternoon at the hospital through the crawl of DC Metro traffic, many emotions rushed through us: confusion, anger, sadness, but also peace.

We picked up the girls from my in-law's house and took them to get ice cream.

We hadn't told them anything about their sister yet, just that we needed to go back for more tests before they could figure out for sure if it was a boy or a girl.

We sat in the car as they ate their ice cream.

Then we drove home.

There would be plenty of time to tell them later.

Managing Hope

In this world you will have trouble, but take heart!
I have overcome the world.
John 16:33

We checked in with each other frequently, just to make sure we were both still on board with our decision not to freak out about what was happening.

"Are you really going to be okay if she doesn't make it?"

"I think so... Will you?"

"Yeah, I think I'll be okay."

We would keep actively choosing hope, we decided. No matter what. That would be our mantra: keep hoping until there is nothing left to hope for. One day at a time. One breath at a time.

So we found a name for her: Adalynn Ellen Dickerson. Adalynn, "noble one." *Little Adam,* I thought. *She will have his warrior spirit. She will be strong and stubborn like her father. She will fight.* Ellen, after a special woman in my family's history, a young student that lived with us when I was a toddler. My other big sister. *She will have Ellen's courage. She will never give up.*

We laughed when we realized we'd inadvertently made her initials that of a defibrillator, AED, found on little signs posted everywhere, in every hospital, school, and public building, marking the location of a device that can save a life when a heart stops working.

For a while, I thought I might just be in denial.

Had they really said she had less than a 30% chance of making it to her first birthday? Had they really said she may very well die in her first few hours of life? To think this beautiful daughter, so alive inside me, might never draw a single breath.

But I wasn't in denial. What I felt could only be called the peace that passes understanding, something outside my own power. How else could I feel so incredibly grateful, so undeniably joyful?

Nothing seemed serious enough to fight over anymore, so we found kinder ways to speak to each other. We cut each other some much needed slack. We listened to each other. We laughed so hard we couldn't breathe. We held each other every chance we got.

We would put the girls to bed and actually talk, like we used to when we were just good friends, long before we realized we were in love, long before we became the busy parents of two young girls.

Usually it started with a rehashing of what the doctors had told us that day. What did it mean? Was this good news or just not worse news? We talked about possible logistics for the months to come. Who would stay with the girls, who would take care of our dog, would we alternate going to the hospital, would we need to be there 24/7 or were we allowed to come home at all…

The conversation turned to other things: what we thought about the world, about everything that was happening in these crazy times, about God, about our dreams for the future, whatever it held.

The girls seemed content that the constant threat of an argument between Mommy and Daddy had somehow disappeared.

Prayers of thanksgiving filled my heart.

I thanked God for my husband, for his trust and faith that made me feel safe in the face of all the unknowns before us. I knew for certain that whatever happened in the end, things would never return to how they were before. I would remember how he held me when my strength fell short during those long, long months of carrying Adalynn, the natural inquisitiveness of strangers getting the best of my intentions to stay hopeful. There he was, reminding me that God was in control, that we had each other and our girls, that we were strong and even stronger together.

I thanked God for my daughters, for their innocence and health. I would be the best mother I could possibly be and teach them what faith, hope and love look like.

I thanked God for my parents, who listened patiently to all my explanations of what was happening, exactly what the doctors had said, what the plan was now. When I was scared, they comforted me; when I was optimistic, they rejoiced with me. They drove me to Boston, paid for all my meals like I was still their little girl. They sat by my side, that long day of Adalynn's life.

I thanked God for my in-laws, who watched our daughters without question, whenever needed; for my brother and sister, for our family and friends, for how much they all believed in us and never doubted we would stay strong, even when it seemed like they believed in us more than we did ourselves.

I thanked God for all the doctors and nurses trying so very hard to help us.

I thanked God for my employer, who generously allowed me as much time off as needed; for my co-workers, who supported me each day, who cheered with me when I got good news and reassured me when I got more bad news.

I thanked God for our church, our pastor, and all the faithful people I didn't even know who never stopped praying for me, for Adam, for Adalynn.

I thanked God for caring enough to send me His peace, and not just His peace, but also gifts of patience, love and joy.

No, I wasn't in denial.

I was being blessed beyond measure.

As the months wore on and we continued to wait and hope and pray, people would ask how I was managing to "deal with everything so well." I didn't know how to answer that question other than that God gave me the strength and peace I needed.

I hardly understood it myself.

Uncannily, it seemed every time I started to give in to self-pity, I would immediately be presented with some unimaginable story of suffering or loss that restored my sense of perspective.

I found I was surrounded by stories of lost children, by mothers who were in various stages of healing.

An otherwise healthy infant lost at just over a week old due to complications from what is now considered a preventable infection.

A baby lost at 12 weeks to miscarriage, the mother's third miscarriage in as many years.

A teenage son lost to cancer just weeks after his diagnosis.

A mother who'd lost both her adult sons to illness in the past few years.

A baby stillborn at 32 weeks.

A child lost to suicide.

A daughter, 28, who died in her sleep unexpectedly.

A son who was still alive, but lost in his addiction.

A baby girl whose severe birth defects went undiagnosed during her mother's seemingly normal pregnancy. She was resuscitated at least once a day in the eighteen days she fought for life before her mother finally had to make the decision to let her go.

My own mother, who'd lost a baby at four months pregnant. I came along about two years later. What would have happened, I wondered, if that baby had lived?

My heart ached for these mothers, for these people who suddenly opened up to me with their stories of pain and sorrow. If they could find a way to go on, then surely so could I.

Because how could what I felt as I carried Adalynn each day possibly compare to that of a mother who had tried for years to conceive only to face a disease such as this? Could it be worse than having your son, so full of potential and promise, killed in a random act of hatred just days before his graduation? How could it compare to the pain felt by a mother, powerless, holding her child as he dies of starvation, or the mothers in Syria, watching their children convulse in agony from the effects of poison gas after surviving years of brutal civil war? How could it be worse than Mary's pain, after all she'd witnessed, her beloved son brutally crucified on a cross as a criminal, hearing him ask God to forgive *us,* because we didn't know what we were doing?

In light of all this, my pain felt very, very small.

I decided that trusting in God meant more than just accepting my lot, more than just praying for a miracle. It meant I would never give up. I would lift others up whenever I could, encouraging them to hope, to slow down and love their families, to realize how precious life is—all the things that become so clear and obvious when you are faced with something as final as death, as serious as being responsible for trying to save someone's life. All the things that are so easily forgotten when everything

16

is going along as usual, and it seems like there is no need to rely on God for strength and direction.

My hope started to change: from a hope that Adalynn would be miraculously healed to a hope that no matter what happened, God would be glorified. A hope that it would all have been for a reason. Not some random accident without purpose, but something beautiful, that planted hope in other people and brought light to this dark and troubled world. Whether it was through God's amazing healing power or the witness of two parents who refused to give in to despair.

I thought of the hundreds of people praying for my baby, for sweet little Adalynn. It was overwhelming. What if she didn't make it? What would we tell all these people, so faithful in their prayers for healing and hoping for the best?

What if the best turned out to be the scenario where she didn't make it after all?

I too prayed for healing, but I'd also listened to the doctors, watched them draw their pictures of what a heart should look like, what my daughter's heart looked like, why the specific anatomy of her heart made things all the more difficult.

She's a fighter. You're doing everything you can. It will work out somehow, you'll see. Everything happens for a reason.

I saw both outcomes clearly: the one where she lived and the one where she died. *Either way, Lord,* I prayed. *Either way. As long as You are with me, either way.*

If she lived, there would be weeks, months spent in the hospital. What would the girls think? *Mommy has abandoned us for Adalynn.* There would be hospital bills, the question of what to do about my job. Could I work part-time? Could we even afford that? We'd have to. We would keep taking things one day at a time. We would stay strong as a family. We would care for one another.

If she died...

I tried not to think too much about what would happen then. We would continue to thank God for her life, for how she had changed us and brought love back to our home and joy to our hearts.

All we knew for sure was that of all the paths we could have chosen when we got Adalynn's diagnosis— Adam, falling farther into addiction; me, giving into depression and self-pity—we chose hope instead. We would keep choosing hope, day by day, hour by hour, trusting in God and believing in each other.

It was ten days before Adalynn's scheduled delivery date. The girls and I walked out of church into a fine mist and the sweet smell of early summer rain.

Adam was working that Sunday, showing properties to a prospective buyer, trying to get everything wrapped up during the busiest time of year for selling real estate before Adalynn arrived.

"Excuse me," a voice called out from behind us.

I turned to see one of the church members who had recently started attending services again hurrying towards us.

"Are you the pregnant lady we're supposed to be praying for? They said you were having a C-section on the 6th."

Without letting me answer, she went on to explain how there was absolutely nothing to worry about. C-sections were so common these days. She didn't understand what the trouble was.

I took a deep breath, gathering my thoughts. How best to summarize…

The girls stood patiently, one on either side of me, holding my hands. The cool mist was starting to become actual rain.

I told her I really wasn't worried about myself at all. People were praying for us and a smooth delivery on the 6th because our daughter had a very serious heart defect and would need immediate emergency care to help her live once she was born. The doctors had decided that a

C-section delivery would give her the best possible chance of survival.

She was horrified. She hadn't known.

I told her it was okay; we were still very hopeful that everything would turn out fine.

But then she clarified. She was horrified, not because she had so misunderstood the nature of the prayer request offered up on our behalf, but because she, specifically, hadn't been praying for us as well. She explained that she had a very close connection to God, that her prayers had led to several successful miracles in the past. She was a very strong prayer, you see, and she knew just how to ask for a miracle. If only she had known, she would have been praying for us the entire time. Now it was too late.

Her words rang in my ears.

Now it's too late.

I took another deep, deep breath.

Rain began to fall in earnest. I gripped the girls' hands tighter.

"Well, there are already many people praying for us and our baby, and we're very grateful. I'm sure one more couldn't hurt though."

I managed a smile as we turned and walked away from her towards our car.

"Thank you so much for your concern," I called over my shoulder. "I'd better get these girls out of the rain."

I shook my head as we drove away, thinking how the old me would have secretly despised this woman for the rest of my life.

The new me felt only pity.

Forgiveness

It wasn't that things had been so bad before. Except that sometimes they were.

Resentment, blame and mistrust were eating away at the corners of our marriage, creeping into tiny cracks in our foundation and making them grow. *If only I could get more sleep, I could fix all this,* but there was never enough time and the days continued to pass without us fixing anything.

Of course there were good times, and thankfully they far outweighed the bad times. Still, like a disease left untreated, the symptoms were becoming impossible to ignore.

Too many nights ended in Adam drinking way more than he should, me getting angry and starting to nag him, purposefully undermining him in front of our daughters, going to bed with the unsettled feeling that all this was unsustainable, that this is exactly why people get divorced suddenly at twenty years of marriage and no one ever sees it coming. *Such a happy couple! How could this happen?*

I felt so torn. On the surface of things, I had absolutely nothing to complain about. He was a wonderful husband. I had a beautiful family, a comfortable life. And who provided much of that comfortable life? Adam. He mowed the lawn and took care of our house without being asked. He washed the dishes and took out the trash without being reminded. He paid our bills, on time and without complaining. He planned for our future. He gave the girls baths and tickled them and played with them in our backyard. He made dinner when I was late getting home. What more did I want? Why couldn't I just let it go that he was becoming an alcoholic, albeit a highly functioning alcoholic?

But I couldn't let it go.

Because there was the Christmas morning where I opened presents from Santa with our girls *alone* and played with our girls *alone* and ate Christmas breakfast with our girls *alone* and tried to explain to our five year old why Daddy wasn't getting out of bed.

"He's sick," I told her, barely bothering to disguise the bitterness in my voice. "He'll be better soon."

And before that, there was our friend's wedding when I was 37 weeks pregnant with our second daughter. He had promised not to drink "more than a beer or two," just in case, since I was so close to going into labor and we were over an hour away from home.

As we walked out to the parking lot, he stumbled on the stairs and almost knocked me down. He had been holding himself together well, but here he was, absolutely drunk, the drunkest I'd seen him in years. I got him in the car and asked him if he knew the best way to get home. He was useless. I found my way to the highway, cursing my GPS for not working precisely when I needed it to, my fury growing, fueled by end-of-pregnancy hormones and far too many broken promises.

He got sick all over my car.

Again and again.

We made it home somehow.

I helped him out of the car and stripped off his soiled suit in our driveway.

It was after 1:00 a.m. I didn't care what the neighbors thought. I was screaming at him; so angry, I was shaking.

I got him inside, up the stairs, into the shower.

Don't go into labor right now.

Just breathe. Breathe.

I turned on the shower, ice cold. He was so out of it, he barely flinched. I adjusted the water temperature and left him there with the warm water running over him.

"Try not to drown," I spat at him.

I would never forgive him.

But in the morning, he got up, cleaned the car, took his suit to the dry cleaner, apologized over and over. Our little daughter was born just two weeks later and life went on.

Wasn't the world messed up enough to justify drinking excessively? Why couldn't I simply be grateful for all the many ways he was an amazing husband and father? Part of me wanted to forgive him, but the lure of self-pity kept the wounds fresh and unhealed.

What if he was honestly trying his best?

What if it was me that needed to change?

I started to pray a new prayer.

I prayed that God would change my heart, that I would stop worrying every minute that the worst was about to happen and just live. That I would learn to trust Him and His plan for my life without always trying to control everything. That I would love my family and allow myself to be loved.

Send me your joy, Lord, so I can share your light, not add to the darkness.

Nothing happened; things went on as usual.

I kept praying.

Let me see all this from his side, Lord. Help me be humble. Teach me patience.

Compassion crept into my heart and began to change my perspective.

I saw how he might view his life lately: His wife is so angry and has been angry *for years.* Nothing he does helps. It only makes things worse. He can't even touch her without her flinching half the time. He doesn't understand it. No matter how hard he tries, it just goes on and on and on. *I'm doing everything I can. I'm so sorry.*

I thought of all the years that I had loved this man. Of everything we had been through. Of all the times I had desperately needed forgiveness. Of how freely he gave it, time after time.

I thought of the evening so many years earlier, when we sat together, watching the sun set over the Pacific Ocean. The sun lit up the sky in impossibly beautiful colors, the fading light bouncing off the low clouds, reddening the beach below. Adam was 21; I was 20. We were on a cross-country adventure to see America, as far from home as we could be. We were young and stupid and in love.

We turned at the sound of voices rising over the dunes and watched a middle-aged woman hurriedly make her way across the dim beach. Her presumed husband followed along at a more patient pace as she stumbled through the loose sand in her high heels. She stopped and flung off her shoes with irritation. She ran to the shoreline, calling over her shoulder with determination and a life's measure of frustration: "I done come 3,000 miles to stick my feet in the Pacific Ocean! Ain't nothin' gonna stop me now!"

The woman plunged her bare toes into a surging wave, then immediately turned around and walked back towards her husband, muttering to herself. We watched her husband, standing calmly, arms crossed over his chest, smiling gently, waiting for his wife to find her discarded shoes.

"You think it's a little colder than she thought?" Adam whispered.

I giggled quietly. "Probably so."

"Well, I guess they'll just go back home now," Adam declared facetiously.

I leaned my head back against his chest, laughing, imagining a future still to be lived, one day at a time. How young we were. How full of hope and dreams.

I realized now what I had always missed in that story. At the time, I thought it was remarkable because we had witnessed this unknown woman's private moment of triumph, whatever it meant for her and whatever had led her to that place that evening.

Now I saw the beauty behind that scene really lay in the husband's patient response to his wife's frantic rush across the empty beach. He didn't judge her or make any comment. He just loved her for who she was.

Nearly fifteen years later, I was home alone, waiting for Adam so we could leave for our appointment at the hospital.

We were excited to find out later that day whether we would be welcoming a baby boy or girl to our family in June. We joked about our appointment being on Friday the 13th—shouldn't we reschedule?—and how I was considered "high-risk" due to my "advanced maternal age" of 35. I certainly didn't feel high-risk. Minus a few minor bouts of morning sickness, I felt better than I had in years.

Our daughters were thrilled about the new addition coming to our family, especially if it could please, please, please be a sister.

We had enjoyed a wonderful Christmas.

I was just starting to feel the baby's first flutters and kicks.

There was peace in our home.

Everything was working out perfectly.

As I waited, I paused by our front door and read for the hundredth time the two little blue notecards I had placed there a few months earlier as a reminder to myself whenever I left the house:

This is the day the Lord has made.
Let us *rejoice* and be glad in it!

Pray without ceasing!

I smiled and thanked God for this day, so full of promise and joy. I thanked Him for my husband, for my beautiful daughters, for this child inside me. I prayed that God would keep changing my heart, that I would keep living this new life I was discovering, day by day. I began begging God to protect Adam, to bless him, to show me how to love him as he deserved to be loved—not for the man he used to be or whoever I thought he should be, but for who he was *now*, in this moment. To honestly and truly love him and support him, to accept once and for all that I cannot and should not change him, that he is perfect just as he is, a special child of God.

I felt so content in that moment: a quiet morning on a sunny winter day, standing alone in my cozy little house, my hands on my stomach, surrounding my sweet baby that would soon be here, waiting for my husband whom I loved and cherished to come home.

Forgiveness was possible. Grace was real.

Lessons in Waiting

The girls had lots of questions about what their little sister would be like when she finally arrived.

"Can I give Adalynn this book when she comes home?"

I'm not sure if she'll ever get to come home.

"Definitely," I answered. "She'll love it!"

"Will she like Mickey Mouse?"

"Oh, she'd better!"

Would I ever get to lazily watch cartoons with her on Saturday mornings? Would I ever take those mornings for granted?

"What color eyes do you think she'll have?"

I may never see her eyes.

"Hmmm, maybe hazel, like yours?"

"Yeah, I think they'll be hazel."

"What should she be for Halloween?"

"I'm not sure."

"Can she be a flower so we can be butterflies?"

She'll be almost five months old by then. We'll be getting ready for her second open-heart surgery. I'll have to be in the hospital with her during both the girls' birthdays and Christmas...

"Why are you crying, Mommy?"

I told them again about Adalynn. That she was going to be very sick when she was born. That her heart wasn't working quite right, and the doctors weren't sure if they could fix it, but they were going to try as hard as they could. That we were going to be a family and help each other. Everything was going to be fine, no matter what happened. God had a plan for us, and we just had to wait and see what was going to happen.

"Mommy, why did God only give Adalynn half a heart?"

"I don't know, Sweetie. I don't know."

I cried: tears of joy, that my daughters already loved their sister so very much, and sadness, that Adalynn would most likely never get to meet them.

The days and weeks crept by, ever so slowly. We continued to wait and see what would happen, to promise each other we would not lose hope. We would do whatever was possible to try and save her. You need us to go to Boston? Fine, we'll go to Boston. You need me to do another two hour MRI? No problem, just tell me when to be there.

We knew the reality of how small her chances were, but there was a chance, so we would keep going. Step by step. Day by day. Following the plan. Doing whatever was needed to give her the best possible chance. This was my comfort: that I would never look back and say, *If only I had done this* or *If only I had tried that.*

I learned as much as I could about the disease. I read again and again about blood oxygen levels being persistently low in babies with HLHS and a severely restrictive or intact atrial septum. About mortality rates being significantly higher in these cases. I read that congenital heart defects are present in about 1% of births each year. Of that 1%, hypoplastic left heart syndrome makes up about 5 to 9% of those defects. Of that 5 to 9%, approximately 6 to 11% have the added complication of a highly restrictive or intact atrial septum, where the opening that should be present between the left and right atria during fetal development is either very small or absent altogether. I wasn't really sure what all that meant in terms of actual numbers, other than that this was rare and very serious.

I kept waiting.

I began to see how my prayers for God to teach me patience were being answered. All the hours spent waiting—in doctor's offices, at the hospital, in conference rooms, waiting for the results of the latest tests—gave me more than enough opportunity to slow down and *think*, something I hadn't really taken time to do in quite a while. Between working full-time and raising two little girls, it seemed I barely had a chance to sleep, let alone ponder God's mysterious ways.

Now, suddenly, here was all this time.

Time to just think.

I was usually too nervous at my appointments to do more than sit there quietly. Flipping randomly through a magazine. Smiling at people. Trying to make the receptionist's day brighter, not worse. Watching the other patients, the parents and children, the tiny infants, imagining what journeys they were on.

The hours lying motionless inside the MRI tube gave me the most time to think without interruption as I listened to the patterns of sound—the series of sustained beeps, the short, high-pitched squeals, the long pauses followed by the sudden deep, resonate booms—wondering what they meant, how they could possibly tell the doctors anything about my baby's lungs or brain, feeling Adalynn moving, rolling and kicking when she was supposed to be staying still and cooperating for the radiologist.

My little fighter.

I thought about Adalynn, what she might be like. *How long would it be before I could hold her? Would they even let me see her before they took her to the Cath Lab? How was I going to handle all this?*

One day at a time. One breath at a time.

That's all we ever have, I realized. One moment at a time in which to live our lives. How often we forget how precious each moment is in our hurry to get things done, to get ahead, and plan for the future. As if that future were somehow guaranteed! As if it all couldn't just end at any time: a random car crash, a sudden illness, a tragic accident, a gruesome terrorist attack. When your future is suddenly exposed as uncertain and unknowable, each moment of each day becomes a gift, not a guarantee.

These had been the longest months of my life, but I felt grateful to have been set on this path. As I started to live moment by moment, truly trusting that God was leading me and was in control, how simple things became. There was no more need for worry. I loved more deeply and forgave more readily. I found myself placed in situations where I could share some of God's light with this dark world. I felt God's presence in everything I did, every life I touched, and I realized He had been there all along. I just wasn't paying attention.

In trying to offer me guidance during those long months of waiting for Adalynn, my mother told me one day: there will be mountaintop-type experiences in life, where everything seems so clear, where we are given a glorious view of God's perspective, a glimpse of how it all fits together. But we can't stay on that mountaintop forever. The valley is where we must live and work and learn to trust that God is in control.

And what I have learned on my journey is that part of that trust means accepting, even if we are stuck in the deepest of valleys, that the mountaintop view is still there and always has been and always will be. It does not depend on our eyes seeing it to exist. It is always there, waiting for us to discover and rediscover it.

I had forgotten in my busy life how very little power I actually had to control anything. I'd had my plans all laid out. This baby would be a little boy and would complete our family perfectly. We could stop debating if we should have another child or just enjoy the two beautiful daughters we already had. I had a name all picked out in my mind. I'd dug up the baby boy clothes I kept tucked away in a box in the attic, just in case.

But God, it turns out, had another plan in mind.

I thought for sure we would lose her in Boston.

I was twenty-six weeks pregnant. Our fetal cardiologist had consulted with the specialists at Boston Children's Hospital, and it seemed a fetal cardiac intervention was Adalynn's best chance at being strong enough to survive the emergency catheterization she'd need immediately after birth to open up a passage between her left and right atria. Without this opening, the doctor told us, there would be no path for the blood returning from her lungs to leave the left atrium. Blood would back up into her lungs. No oxygen would be able to reach her organs or her brain.

I allowed his words to register.

In recent years, he explained, specialized teams of doctors like the group at Boston Children's, had started trying to create an opening in the atrial septum in utero. This was to *hopefully* improve the odds that babies with this type of defect would survive not only the catheterization immediately after birth, but the multiple surgeries needed in their first few months of life. Unfortunately, there simply weren't enough cases of this rare condition for them to be able to say with any degree of certainty whether their attempts had technically been successful or not. It *seemed* to help, which was reason enough for us to decide it was worth the risk.

There was about a 50% chance that the procedure would make any difference. There was about a 10% chance that the procedure itself could kill her, or make me go into pre-term labor, which would lead to the same result.

My parents traveled with me to Boston while Adam stayed home with the girls.

We arrived in the early evening on Tuesday, March 7. My parents politely ignored the fact that the hotel I selected because of its reasonable "patient rate" was directly across the street from a Methadone Clinic. Drug addicts of all sorts roamed the parking lot of the hotel and neighboring gas station. Sirens blared outside the window throughout the night.

We spent our first day at Boston Children's meeting with all the different specialists that would be involved in the procedure, so they could assess me and make sure I completely understood what was happening and hadn't changed my mind after they reviewed all the risks.

Yes, I understand. Yes, I still want to go forward with it.

We met with the obstetrician from Brigham and Women's Hospital, the neighboring hospital where the delicate procedure would be performed the next day and where I would be kept overnight for observation. Working along with doctors from Boston Children's Advanced Fetal Care Center, she would use an ultrasound to position Adalynn perfectly so that a small needle could be placed by another doctor through my abdomen and into Adalynn's heart.

We met with the anesthesiologist and reviewed the plan for the following day, discussed the risks involved in any form of sedation, how members of the anesthesia team would be monitoring me and Adalynn the entire time. Adalynn would need to be given a medicine to paralyze her temporarily. Would I like to take something to help me stay calm during the procedure?

As I lay in the operating room the next morning, numb from the waist down, strapped to a table, being pivoted repeatedly from side to side, back and forth, up and down, as they tried and tried to get Adalynn to roll over, I suddenly realized why some people chose to be sedated for this. Still, I was glad I had declined their offer. I wanted to be fully aware. I watched the bustle of medical professionals going about their tasks, making sure everything was in order so they could begin, the young anesthesia interns struggling to get a make-shift curtain to stay in place to block my view of what was happening. Every time the curtain started to fall, I caught a glimpse of Adalynn on the large monitor the OB was using to get her in the proper position. I could see her heart, beating rapidly on the screen. I saw her face, the outline of her tiny nose. Eventually, one of the anesthesia techs was assigned the job of holding up the curtain for the duration of the procedure.

We met with the Fetal Cardiologist and the rest of the Boston team. He drew the pictures I could draw by memory at that point on a large whiteboard. Here is a normal heart. Here is what a hypoplastic heart looks like. Here is what your daughter's heart looks like. Here is what we are going to try to do tomorrow. Here are all the reasons why we may not be successful. Do you have any questions?

My father, in his special way of dealing with stressful situations with a mixture of humor and practicality, paused for just the briefest of moments before saying: "I do have one question, actually. If there is no left side of the heart and there's only a right ventricle, shouldn't it just be called *the* ventricle?" The cardiologist looked to me in confusion. I smiled at him. It wasn't the first time my father had left someone speechless.

No, we don't have any questions. Yes, I still want to go forward with the procedure.

My last meeting of the day was with the hospital's resident neonatologist. We had already been at the hospital for over eight hours that day and were all ready to get some rest and prepare for the morning. His small office was very cramped, so my parents opted to wait for me in the lobby.

I wasn't exactly clear on why I was being asked to meet with a neonatologist. Wasn't that a doctor that took care of premature babies? *Maybe I missed something,* I thought as I waited for him to arrive. When he walked in, I noted he had a sort of tracheal tube in his neck that neither of the two nurses in the room with us made any mention of as he explained his role at the hospital and how premature babies are generally cared for.

He spoke his words kindly, carefully.

There was an audible sound of air going through the trach after each phrase.

We just want to make sure.
    Breath sound.
You are fully aware.
    Breath sound.
That if you go into labor.
    Breath sound.
Or the baby is in distress.
    Breath sound.
There is nothing that can be done.
    Breath sound.
To save her.
    Breath sound.
        Breath sound.
            Breath sound.

Yes, I understood. I understood everything. Yes, I still wanted to go forward with the procedure.

My parents and I went back to our hotel and waited for it to be time to leave for the hospital in the morning.

I don't recall if I slept or not that night.

But Adalynn did make it through the intervention.

After trying for almost ninety minutes to get her in position, the doctors decided to call off the procedure. She was not cooperating. They would need to allow the paralytic to fully wear off and then try again the next day. I would stay in the hospital overnight and be taken back to the OR in the morning. They were hopeful they would have better luck on their second attempt.

The next morning they repeated the same steps as the previous day. The epidural was put in place; they tested my abdomen with a cold towel to make sure I had no feeling; my arms were strapped to the operating table; they placed a pair of headphones over my ears to block out the sounds, to give me something soothing to focus on. This time they had two poles ready to attach the curtain to so it would stay firmly in place. By luck, or by accident, the way they positioned the curtain gave me a full view of the ultrasound monitor. I could see the familiar images, the red and blue blurs, the rush of colors mixing, that somehow represented the blood flowing through Adalynn's tiny heart.

The unique shape of her atrial septum had made the procedure nearly impossible. They were able to make a small, 3 mm hole, but that was the best that could be done.

The nurses came every few hours that day and throughout the night to check for Adalynn's heartbeat. She was doing just fine, they assured me. I was finally discharged on Saturday afternoon.

We left Boston at 4:30 p.m. and my father, who had just celebrated his 73rd birthday, drove for 7 ½ hours straight back to my parents' house in Delaware.

I looked out the window, wrapped my arms tightly around my abdomen, watched the cities come and go as we drove down I-95.

Afternoon turned to evening.

My father kept driving. My mother never once questioned him when he almost drove off the road or let the speedometer creep up to 95 mph.

We got to their house just after 12:00 a.m.

She waited patiently while my father searched for the house keys he had somehow misplaced when we'd left on Tuesday.

I wanted to learn to love like that.

In the morning I woke up early, anxious to get back home to Adam and the girls. I snuck up to my parents' room to say goodbye.

They were both still sound asleep, exhausted by the long trip, the long week spent waiting in the hospital, the worry over their daughter, their granddaughter.

I watched them sleeping for a while, thinking how very lucky I was to have parents like these kind people. I left a note on their desk and started back home to Maryland.

We waited to see if the hole would stay or not.

By mid-April, just four weeks after the procedure, the hole had closed back up to its original size. There was nothing more to do but keep waiting, praying that her lungs would not be too damaged before she was ready to be born.

The week before our scheduled C-section date, I took off work to rest and prepare.

I tried my best to stay calm, focusing my energy on things like making frozen meals, organizing our kitchen drawers, cleaning out closets, repotting all our houseplants.

I packed a bag for the girls to stay at my in-laws' house. I didn't know how long we would be gone.

Three days? Three weeks? Three months?

There were no baby clothes to wash and fold. There was no nursery to decorate, no car seat to install. We had plenty of time to do those things later, if we needed to.

The days went by, one by one.

Lord, protect little Adalynn. Please, help her be strong.

Adam and I arrived at Washington Hospital Center as planned on the evening of June 5. The nurses hooked me up to the fetal heart monitor and applauded Adalynn's strong heartbeat.

"Stronger than some of the healthy babies we see," they told me. "She's a fighter. She'll be just fine."

Our C-section was scheduled for 6:30 a.m. the following morning, next door at Children's Hospital.

How long that night was as I watched the hour hand of the hospital clock slowly, slowly, slowly makes its way towards 5:00 a.m. when the high-risk OB was scheduled to come pick us up to walk us over to Children's for the surgery.

He showed us the path: out of the unit, down the elevators, down a long hallway, follow the signs for MRI, out the back door of the hospital, down the ramp, through a small parking lot, around past the emergency entrance, into Children's Hospital. This is the way I could go later when I was feeling up to visiting Adalynn. Adam would stay with her at Children's while I recovered from the C-section back at Washington Hospital Center.

I got checked in at Children's. My parents waited with us until it was time to go into the Operating Room.

My epidural was in place; my legs were numb.

It was time.

Lying on that table, the doctors, nurses and anesthesia team moving quickly all around me, getting everything ready, Adam, holding my hand, time ticked away, closer and closer to the moment when she would have to come out.

I thought of the procedure in Boston, how eerily similar this scene was.

Couldn't she stay in a little longer? Just another hour? A few more minutes?

"You'll feel a little pressure," the OB called out from the other side of the curtain.

And then, there was her cry.

When I heard Adalynn cry out as she took her first breath, that breath the doctors weren't sure she would be able to take or not, hope flooded through me.

Adam and I locked eyes. That strong cry—that has to be a good sign!

They held Adalynn up to show her to Adam, then quickly took her away to the Cath Lab. I wouldn't see her face until she was lying peacefully in the CICU.

They took me back over to Washington Hospital Center through a dimly-lit tunnel that ran under the city block. The tunnel was old and rarely used, except in these types of circumstances.

I felt empty, but still so hopeful, remembering the sound of her cry as they pushed my stretcher through that long, winding passageway and back to my room, the same room I had spent the night before, counting the hours until my baby would be born.

I tried to rest as I was told to. I would need to be strong for Adalynn in the days to come. Now was the time to rest.

As the hours passed, I felt increasingly powerless in that small hospital room. I couldn't stop staring at the clock on the wall in front of me. I tried to make some kind of small talk with my parents, waiting patiently with me by my bedside. I tried to stay calm, to focus on my breathing, to ignore the painful contractions that came and went every few minutes. I wanted to jump out of the bed and run to her, fighting somewhere in the hospital next door. I wanted to be with Adam. But I couldn't run. I couldn't even sit up on my own.

The nurses came in periodically to check on me, to press on my abdomen, and ask me how I was feeling.

Yes, I'm sure I don't want anything else for pain. I just want to go see my baby, please. 7 PM? I can't wait that long. Please, please, can't you speak with the doctor again?

My heart sank when Adam entered the room unexpectedly around 11:30 a.m., followed by the fetal cardiologist and the nurse who had coordinated all our care since our first visit to Children's in January.

This can't be good. I searched Adam's eyes.

What had happened?

The doctor sat down on the edge of the bed.

This definitely can't be good.

She told me they were having difficulty with the catheterization. There was a lot of bleeding, but Adalynn was stable for the moment.

I started breathing again.

She said they had almost lost her, they had started CPR, they'd done everything they could to revive her, but there was too much bleeding. She had just started to tell Adam the sad news when a nurse rushed out to the waiting room to say the bleeding had stopped. Inexplicably. Adalynn was still alive!

My mother and I looked at each other. *Inexplicably?* So this was God's miracle! He had stopped the bleeding. She had all but died and come back. She was alive!

How incredible! I would choose to focus my attention on this bit of information, not on everything else that seemed to be going wrong.

Adam returned to Children's. The plan now was to let Adalynn rest while they regrouped and tried to come up with another method to get her atrial septum open. They would need about two hours to finish stabilizing Adalynn so she could be moved to the Cardiac Intensive Care Unit (CICU). They would clean her up, and then Adam could go in to see her.

I dozed off for a while, comforted in knowing my precious daughter had been saved.

Serendipity

Our pastor came to visit me while I waited in my room for more news. He had just left Adam after seeing Adalynn settled into the CICU at Children's. I was grateful for his calm presence as we talked about Adalynn's amazing recovery from the point of death, about all that had led up to this day. Adam, he assured me, was holding up very well.

As we talked, I wondered at his use of the word "serendipity" at several points in our conversation.

How curious, I thought. Wasn't serendipity when something unexpectedly *good* happened? A pleasant surprise or a happy accident, like discovering penicillin or two former lovers randomly meeting on a busy street, just when both happened to be unattached? But serendipity was more than just a happy coincidence. It was when you were searching for something and along the way, you *just so happened* to discover something else completely, something wonderful, something entirely unpredictable that changed everything.

None of this was exactly serendipitous.

Or was it?

It was mid–February.

We'd weighed our options and had decided to go forward with the fetal cardiac intervention at Boston Children's Hospital.

As I finalized my plans for the trip, I hesitantly drafted an email to an old friend who just so happened to live in Boston. I kept my message short, not mentioning the actual reason for my visit, cautiously asking if he might possibly be around the first week of March. I held my breath and clicked send. Would he even respond? To my delight, he replied within minutes. He would love to see me! He had space on his couch just for me to crash if I needed a place to stay. He would be studying for finals a few days that week, but otherwise he was fully available.

I breathed a sigh of relief. I had been hesitant because I hadn't actually spoken to this friend in several years. We had slowly lost touch, my last messages going unreturned completely. And although the rational part of my mind knew for certain that he was just busy with medical school, researching new ways to treat cancer, and life in general, the rest of me worried that maybe he had finally gotten fed up with me and had deliberately moved on.

This wasn't just any friend who *just so happened* to live in Boston and *just so happened* to have completed his first year of residency at the very same hospital I would be staying in. This was someone I had gone to high school and college with, someone who had graciously taken me to our senior prom when I found myself without a date. This was someone who had put up with me waking him up at 3:00 a.m. during college because I simply couldn't sleep or had inadvertently deleted a 25-page term paper that was due the next morning. Someone who had seen me at my best and at my very worst. This was the person I had asked to be called when I was taken to the hospital late one night for a possible overdose. He came immediately, without question or judgment. Of all the people that could have *just so happened* to live in Boston, it was this friend.

I thanked him for his kind offer of a place to stay and filled him in on my actual reason for traveling to Boston. He was reassuring as always, and promised to come visit me whenever I got settled in at the hospital.

He sat with me for hours, keeping me company, talking about our lives, our families, the current state of the American healthcare system, how it was hopelessly broken, what is was like to have children, as well as all the precise details of what the doctors had told me, what they had tried to do that morning to help Adalynn, what they would try again to do the next day.

The questions we didn't address were: Would they be successful this time? Would they accidentally kill her? Would it make any difference?

And it was just as I'd thought. He had in fact just been busy living his own life. He held no ill-will, no grudges. This fear I had been harboring was suddenly gone forever.

Maybe our pastor was right to use that word after all. *Serendipity.*

Hadn't Adalynn brought joy to our lives in so many unexpected ways? Hadn't we found forgiveness where there was once anger and worry? Hadn't we finally learned to live a life based on faith and trust, praying without ceasing, not blindly, carelessly pushing through each day, but rejoicing, deliberately, in the gifts that God had made?

It had all started with a prayer, or the beginnings of a prayer.

The stirring of a heart longing for change.

For peace.

How could we know how one thing would lead to another, how lives would be touched, how hope would spread?

Maybe these were the secret discoveries God laid out for us as He drew up His plans to redirect us along a better path: a marriage healed, an old friendship renewed, a heart transformed into a beacon of light.

And what if something as simple as just one mother stopping to look at her teenage daughter and really seeing her for the first time in a long while and taking time to hug her, to really hold her—what if that was purpose enough?

One Sunday in May, just a few weeks before Adalynn's scheduled delivery date, our regular pastor was out of town. That Sunday, a visiting pastor preached a sermon on the history of miraculous healing in the Bible, outlining the various ways healing was described in the Gospel and making his case for why we should continue to pray for one another and believe in the healing power of prayer.

After the service, several well-meaning people encouraged me to take advantage of the healing prayer time that the pastor had offered to anyone who was interested.

I felt overwhelmed and declined as politely as possible. There was no way I could bring myself to be that vulnerable, but maybe I should listen to them.

Maybe they were right.

It was all so pointless, wasn't it?

Such a human reaction to try to control things—as if this man could actually heal my baby.

But what if he could?

We didn't want to dampen everyone's hopes with more bad news, so we hadn't said anything to the congregation that Sunday.

What none of them knew was that we had just received the MRI results we'd been waiting for all week since the latest round of tests. We knew Adalynn's heart still looked about the same as the last scan, but we'd gotten no definitive word on her lungs. We'd learned by this point that it is never a good sign when doctors want to have other specialists "review the results" before they tell you what they are seeing. So, after waiting four full days for an update, we'd found out that Friday afternoon that Adalynn's lungs were most likely full of fluid.

We didn't know for sure what this meant, other than that it made it all the more probable that she would be extremely unstable at birth, that she may need to be put immediately on the ECMO machine the doctors had described in detail during our last visit. There was simply no way to know for certain, the doctors told us, until she was born and tried to take a breath.

Was this visiting pastor, so confident in his assertions that miraculous healing was still possible in our modern age, here this Sunday by mere accident? Was it a gift from God?

I didn't know.

We left church that day, the four of us hand in hand. At home, I fed the girls lunch and then closed the door to our bedroom.

I wept until I fell asleep.

Lord, I believe! Help my unbelief!

A Father's Dream

Adam came downstairs one morning in late March with a look of astonishment.

"I met Adalynn."

"What?"

"I had a dream last night. She was there—I guess it was Heaven."

"What did she look like?"

"She was so beautiful. She was eleven or twelve with long, golden-brown hair. She held out her hand to me and said, 'Daddy, it's me. It's Adalynn.'"

I held Adam's hand and waited for him to go on.

"It was like she was telling me, it's okay, you don't need to worry anymore, about anything. I promise I'll be here, waiting for you."

He smiled, remembering.

"She was so perfect, like an angel."

It was a beautiful dream.

At 2:01 p.m. on June 6, Adam texted me to say he was with Adalynn. After working on her continuously since she was born at 7:15 a.m. that morning, they had gotten her stable enough to allow him in to see her. A close friend of Adam's and our pastor were there with him.

Later that evening, as we sat in my hospital room, the daylight fading away until it was completely dark, he told me what it was like, watching little Adalynn surrounded by nurses and doctors, tubes and wires coming out of her neck, her chest, her arms and legs.

Her chest had been cut open and a clear, plastic bandage covered her midsection, from her neck down to her waist. There were ice packs around her head to try to minimize the swelling and possible brain damage.

By 2:30 the team's pace began to increase. Something was happening.

The nurse said they would need Adam to go back out to the waiting room, but he had a few minutes before they were going to get started.

Adalynn was losing too much blood, the doctor told him. They would need to open her back up to try to stop the bleeding.

Adam whispered in her ear, touching her forehead gently. *Daddy loves you. Mommy loves you. Your sisters love you.*

There was still hope.

A trail of dried blood ran down her neck; dried blood clung to her lips.

Her heartrate increased on the monitor as he spoke to her. She must know he's there. This sweet baby who loved the sound of her father's voice heard through the walls of my belly as he'd told her again and again and again that he loved her. To be strong.

Three coolers, each marked Baby Girl Dickerson, sat in the corner, waiting.

A nurse swiftly opened the cooler closest to Adalynn. They were full of blood packets to be transfused into her tiny body.

"Do you need more blood?" Adam asked, anxious for some tangible way to help. "Can I give some now for her?"

The nurse explained that if he wanted to donate blood, he'd have to go down to the lab. She assured him they had what they needed for Adalynn.

All that blood for our little baby girl.

He kissed her forehead one final time and went out to the waiting room.

Adam's father was on his way to the hospital; he'd be there any minute. His mother would stay home with the girls. His friend headed home, promising to come back again first thing in the morning.

He waited.

The next day, Adam's best friend, Josh, came to take him to get some dinner while I tried to rest. A long walk and some fresh air would do him good. Adam had been amazingly strong, stronger than I'd ever imagined he could be. Stronger than I think I would have been.

At dinner, as they sat at a small table outside a streetside café, the city traffic rushing by, he told Josh the story of seeing Adalynn; how she'd somehow come back to life after the doctors thought they'd lost her that morning; how he got to see her and kiss her tiny cheek, feel her soft skin, hold her tiny hands and feet; how very important it was for him that he had seen her, alive, breathing; how much this precious baby had changed him, had made him understand the fleetingness of this world and how to let go of everything that was cluttering his life and just live each day, trying to make some kind of difference; how the doctor finally, finally came out to the waiting room to say he was sorry. There was too much bleeding. They were not able to save her.

A woman who'd been sitting at the table next to them stood up hesitantly and turned towards them

"I'm so sorry," she said in a lilting Jamaican accent. "I couldn't help but overhear."

She had been enjoying a book and a glass of wine on the warm summer evening as Adam and Josh talked about what you'd expect two people who'd known each other since before they were born to talk about when one of them has just lost a daughter. They laughed and cried and looked at each other with utter seriousness.

The woman apologized again for eavesdropping. "Your story is…so intriguing."

She paused.

She didn't know what to say.

"It's just…it's going to be okay. Everything is going to be okay."

Adam looked up at her.

It felt so right that they were here together at this exact time, at this specific restaurant, the sounds of the city surrounding them.

It was just after 5:00 p.m. on a Wednesday in June. They'd been to two other places that for one reason or another weren't serving actual customers at the moment, so they'd kept walking, traveling over a mile to finally find this streetside café, these two small tables outside the front window.

It felt so right that they were here, and this woman was here, reminding him that life would in fact go on, day by day, one moment, one breath at a time, as it always had.

The question was what to do with those days ahead.

"Can I give you a hug?" Adam asked simply, standing and opening his arms.

And so they stood there, embracing, two strangers; this tall, undefinably masculine, deeply elegant woman; Adam's head resting on her shoulder.

Living

Where does life begin anyway?

At conception? At birth? The date of viability?

Somewhere randomly in between?

I don't know the answer.

Because what if there is never a real guarantee that the baby will be able to live outside the womb? What then?

I think back to the day when the doctor told us that termination was a possible option in our case due to the severity of Adalynn's defect and remain thankful we didn't choose that path.

She was surely alive, kicking and fighting from the moment she could move her limbs.

She kicked and rolled whenever Adam talked to her, pressing his cheek against my growing belly. Little Kicky, we called her.

"Be strong," he'd whisper. "Daddy loves you."

She tasted the best tastes, all my favorite dishes: Thai Green Curry, Eggplant Parmesan, Chana Masala, Family Taco Night.

She felt the excitement of watching play-off hockey with us, as I tried to stay calm enough not to send myself into early labor.

She was with me each day at work, in meetings, providing entertainment for my co-workers as we watched my belly move from side to side.

She was with me in traffic as I drove home, squirming and pushing on my bladder relentlessly.

She was with me everywhere I went, as I answered endless questions from well-meaning strangers—in elevators, in the grocery store, in parking lots. *How far along are you? Is this your first? Oh, your third? Do you know what you're having this time? Another girl? How sweet. Do you think you'll try again for a boy?*

She read stories at bedtime with her sisters. She twisted and turned when she heard the girls laughing and kicked back when they elbowed her accidentally, trying to find a comfortable spot on Mommy's shrinking lap.

She was with me as I lay awake at night, unable to sleep, feeling her push her tiny body against me as I gently pressed on my abdomen.

She knew love.

At 4:15 p.m., my nurse said she had spoken to the doctor, and they had decided they would allow me to go over to Children's now after all, as long as I absolutely promised to stay in my wheelchair and to come back immediately if I started bleeding, felt light-headed, or if my pain increased.

I promised, signed all the necessary documents to release them from liability.

I eased myself carefully into the wheelchair.

The nurse handed me my IV and urinary catheter bag to hold.

As my mother followed along behind us, my father maneuvered my wheelchair down the same path I had traveled that morning: out of the unit, down the elevators, down the long hallway, across the parking lot, through Children's emergency entrance.

Every bump was torture, but I didn't care.

I was getting closer and closer to Adalynn.

How strange it must be for my parents, I thought, returning to the very same hospital I had been admitted to thirty-five years earlier. At five months old, I was diagnosed with hemolytic uremic syndrome, a serious illness that often leads to life-threatening kidney failure. I would likely need a blood transfusion. This was 1982, before they screened for viruses such as HIV in donated blood. A little boy treated in the same unit had in fact contracted the virus, my mother would remind me when she told me the story as a girl. How scared they must have been. Two young children at home. A baby recently lost to miscarriage. Their youngest, just a tiny infant, in the hospital with this strange disease. But my condition improved. I wouldn't need a transfusion after all. I would be fine.

We arrived on the 3rd floor at Children's.

Wait, where is the CICU? None of this looks familiar.

I'd told my dad to take the wrong elevator. We were on the wrong side of the building.

I tried to call Adam. There was no cell service.

A passing nurse gave us directions.

"Not far now. Just follow the signs for the Chaplain."

There it is! There was Adam, waiting for us.

I knew before he spoke.

I was too late.

He knelt down by my wheelchair.

"I'm so sorry, B. Adalynn went home to Heaven about thirty minutes ago."

We held onto each other and just breathed.

In and out. In and out.

What Remains

The day we left the hospital and returned home was a gorgeous 73 degrees with just the slightest of warm Southern breezes and a scattering of puffy white clouds strategically placed across the sky. We sat together on our back porch, holding hands, taking in the beauty of the early-Summer afternoon, waiting for Adam's parents to bring the girls back home.

The days that followed were filled with sunshine and family, music, friends and little girls' laughter.

I kept asking myself: *Why did God choose this path instead? Why didn't He let us at least try? Was life just supposed to go on now?*

So I wrapped up all the necessary details.

I arranged for Adalynn's body to be cremated through a charitable program provided by a local funeral home that donated such services to families at Children's. We picked up her ashes a few weeks later and placed the small white box they gave us in a little basket until we could figure out what to do with it.

I provided the information needed to obtain a birth and death certificate.

I suppressed the milk that came in a few days after I returned home from the hospital.

I managed the onslaught of medical bills and endless explanation of benefits notices.

I put away my maternity clothes.

I removed the emergency contact numbers for the fetal cardiologist and the high-risk obstetrician from my wallet.

I flipped through the blank pages of the journal I'd started to chronicle Adalynn's medical history. My careful lists of doctors, addresses, phone numbers and dates of procedures.

My mother warned me I might feel angry at God.

I didn't believe her.

In the hours and days immediately following Adalynn's birth and death, I thought there was no way this amazing peace I'd felt all these months would simply disappear.

We knew this was the most likely outcome. We'd been given five months to say goodbye to Adalynn.

I knew without a doubt we'd tried everything possible.

I knew that so many people had suffered and were suffering so much more than me.

I knew that Adam and I were stronger than we'd ever been, all because of this precious child.

I knew that God loved us and had a plan for us.

But my mother was right.

Doubts crept in: why had any of this happened? Did it even matter? Would it change anything at all?

I was angry at God. I was very angry.

I was angry that He didn't give me the chance to help Adalynn have a life, to sacrifice and fight and do whatever was needed to keep her alive.

To see her at least once.

There were days full of anguished questions: Had the catheterization killed her? Was there something else they should have done instead? Something else I should have done?

But it wasn't my decision, after all, to determine who lives and who dies.

All the stories I'd been told of tremendous loss flooded my mind. Who was I to sit here moping around feeling sorry for myself? How did that bring any honor to Adalynn's memory or any glory to God?

Still, my feelings of grief were valid.

I, too, had lost a baby. I just lost her slowly, one day at a time, clinging to hope until hope ran out.

I began to accept God's choice.

How could I be angry when He had blessed me in so many ways? Joy and love had been infused back into my marriage. I had a renewed sense of purpose in caring for my daughters—every day with them was special, not to be taken for granted. I now knew, with God's help, just how strong I could be, how much of a difference I could make.

He had, in fact, answered all my prayers, just not in the way I thought He should.

I'd prayed for patience. He gave me the opportunity to learn how to wait with expectation, not wasting away time, but living moment by moment in trust and faith.

I'd prayed for peace. He took away my patterns of destructive thinking, all the worries that were troubling my soul, and taught me how to just be still.

God did protect Adalynn and keep her safe. He did heal her and make her whole, just not how I wanted Him to. Not in this world.

I remembered the prayer I had prayed that Friday morning in January: that God would protect and bless my husband, that I would learn to truly love him, giving up my attempts to control and change him and just accept him as he is. Seeing his strength and faith grow as we walked together on this trying journey, I knew our love would overcome any challenge we may face. I would let God do His work in Adam's life without my interference. I would keep forgiving Adam and I would forgive myself, for all the ways I could never live up to this new life I was being offered. I would allow myself to grieve, but I would not allow the sorrow to consume me.

I would start again, each day, one breath at a time.

I still picture her angelic face, too beautiful to be believed.

She looked so peaceful, lying in the center of the CICU room. All the wires, tubes and pumps had been removed. There was no trace left of the chaos that must have filled that space less than an hour before. I held her, wrapped in the softest pink blanket. A pink knit cap was tucked over her head. Someone had dressed her and wrapped her in a blanket to make it easier for me to see her. Someone had wiped away all the blood and cleaned her perfect face. I said thank you for that person, who had to go home and tell his or her family that there was a baby girl lost during the shift. How the parents were there. And the grandparents. How it was really sad.

I held her close, deep sobs building in my chest, kept in check by the painful incision across my abdomen. Her spirit was already gone, that vivacious, ever-moving life I had carried inside me. I held her tiny body and imagined that she was only sleeping, that she would stir at any moment, making the sweet coos and gurgles little infants make.

But she didn't. She was gone.

I didn't know how to stop holding her.

Was it too soon? Should I hold her longer? How long had I been in this moment?

I handed her to Adam and watched as he cradled her to his chest, watched the love in his eyes for this lost daughter.

I watched my mother say goodbye to this precious granddaughter she had prayed for each day so devotedly.

I watched my father and father-in-law give manly hugs to Adam, encouraging him, strengthening him.

I spoke to my sister, who had been answering questions all day from family and friends about what was happening, what the latest update was, and assured her it was okay she couldn't be there, that I loved her.

I spoke to my mother-in-law, at home alone with the girls, building them an intricate dollhouse out of cardboard boxes to keep her mind busy, waiting for news. I asked her to tell them that their sister had to go back to Heaven, but she loved them and we loved them and we would see them very soon. That everything was going to be okay.

And then there was nothing left to do but turn around and leave the room, leave the unit, leave the hospital, go back through the parking lot, back down the long hallway, back up the elevator, back to my room.

As time passes, sadness and grief ease into gratitude: that she will never feel any pain, that she will never have to face surgery after surgery, a life spent waiting to see when her heart will finally give out.

I don't know if I could have handled having a daughter like Adalynn, but I was prepared to give it my very all.

What remains is the love she brought to our lives. The sort of love that is patient and kind. That keeps no record of wrongs. That forgives. That always protects, always trusts, always hopes, always perseveres.

A love that will never fail.

And now these three remain: faith, hope and love.

*But the greatest of these is **love**.*

Acknowledgement

Thank you to all of you who helped me bring this book to life – who read my drafts and gave me the confidence to keep going. Thank you to Erick Pfleiderer for creating the perfect cover. Thank you to my dear parents, for your tireless support and encouragement. And thank you most of all to my sweet husband, for helping me tell our story and loving me all along the way.